# THE "A" BOOK

A COLLECTION OF SATIRICAL COMMENTS
AND ILLUSTRATIONS ABOUT AUTISM

WRITTEN & ILLUSTRATED
BY
## CARISSA MORDENO PACCERELLI

EMBRY PUBLISHING

Copyright © 2017 Carissa Paccerelli

ISBN-10: 0-9994290-0-0

ISBN-13: 978-0-9994290-0-6

All rights reserved. No part of this book may be used, reproduced, or transmitted in any form or by any electronic or mechanical means, including photocopying, recording, or by any information storage and retrieval system, without written permission from the author and/or publisher, except where permitted by law.

Embry Publishing

Printed in the United States of America

First Paperback Edition

## DEDICATION

Dedicated to my family and friends
who help me survive
in the "A" world.

# THE "A" BOOK

## INTRODUCTION

———

When I was 15 years old, I wrote and illustrated a zine with the same title as this book. Zine, short for magazine or fanzine, is a self-published work of original texts and images. My zine was a collection of satirical comments and illustrations about autism. It received good feedback from family and friends as well as the autism community, which inspired me to make it into a book.

According to the American Psychiatric Association, Autism Spectrum Disorder (ASD) is a complex developmental disorder that can cause problems with thinking, feeling, language, and the ability to relate to others. It is a neurological disorder, which means it affects the functioning of the brain. Autism differs from person to person in its severity, effects, and combinations of symptoms. There is a great range of abilities and characteristics of children with ASD - no two children appear or behave the same way. Symptoms can range from mild to severe and often change over time.[1]

I was diagnosed with ASD when I was six years old. I have a younger brother, George, who was diagnosed when he was two years old. After we received this diagnosis, our parents immediately enrolled us in various programs from special education classes to thousands of therapy hours in speech, occupational, behavioral, and social skills. They put us on a special diet and engaged us in various adaptive recreational activities such as swimming, hockey, surfing, kayaking, bowling, sailing, and even co-piloting a plane. Honestly, I didn't enjoy the majority of these programs.

---

[1]American Psychiatric Association (www.psychiatry.org)

# THE "A" BOOK

My parents were advised by the professionals to keep us busy at all times and not to leave us in our "own little world". Through those years, we have encountered different people. Those who know and understand autism, pretend to know autism, or those who simply wonder if autism is a "real" disability. As annoying as it was, I kind of grew numb to some of it and often joked about those people to my friends who are in the spectrum.

I hope this book will bring enjoyment to people, especially those affected by autism. I hope I don't offend anyone. This book is based on my personal experience and on my autistic friends and family, especially my brother who is non-verbal. This book is dedicated to him.

# I'M A PERSON, NOT A PUZZLE

Am I an "Autistic Person" or
"Person with Autism"?
Is there a difference?
I get confused.
Others get offended.
I don't.
Does it matter?

You can call me either way.
But don't call me a tragedy.
Don't call me rude.
Don't call me oversensitive.

Some says blue is the color of autism.
Blue doesn't represent me.
Doesn't feeling blue means sadness?
I'm bursting in many colors.

I don't have a disease.
So don't try to cure me.
I am a person.
Not a puzzle.
I may be different.
Aren't we all?

THE "A" BOOK

"My Own Little World"

"You don't look autistic!"

# THE "A" BOOK

"You look so happy to be autistic."

"Autistic people are creatures with no empathy for others."

# THE "A" BOOK

"It's okay. I went through this at your age, too."

THE "A" BOOK

# "Happy Stimming"

"Your hands are too loud!
SHUT THEM UP!"

# THE "A" BOOK

"There are two types of autistics:
Those who hug too much
and those who hate it."

THE "A" BOOK

"Your autism is not an excuse for your problems."

"How to get more LIKES in social media."

THE "A" BOOK

"You're such a LUCKY mom!"

"You're autistic, so I'm sure you know who she is."

"It's not like I was going to touch him."

"Because you're autistic, you are somehow blessed with a secret God-like talent no normal neurotypical person can have."

THE "A" BOOK

# "Don't go near that Special Ed kid. He's dangerous."

"Every Autism movie…"

"Refusal and doubt"

"Surely, Yoga can cure this autism you have."

"Do this work! Keep going!"
(while breathing down my neck)

"Baby Talk"

"Born with a tragedy"

"Everyone's the same"

"I think I'm autistic, because all my buddies think I'm so random and weird."

"You're not autistic.
You have feelings and emotions."

# THE "A" BOOK

WELL -I- DON'T THINK YOU HAVE <u>AUTISM</u>!

You're so...

**PRETTY**  **SMART**
**TALENTED**  **NICE**

YOU HAVE... FEELINGS!

"Didn't raise us right."

"You're autistic? I've seen [insert title of show or movie with autistic characters in it]. Have you seen it?"

# THE "A" BOOK

THE "A" BOOK

"Confusing dog training with just asking if you need to pee."

WHAT DO YOU WANT? WHAT DO WANT? SAY "I...WANT... BAAA— THROOM", OK? SAY IT WITH ME: "III— WAAAAAANT—— ..."

"That's so retarded!"

"What you're saying doesn't make sense."

# "Pacing"

# THE "A" BOOK

"Sensory overload at a party"

# THE "A" BOOK

"Are you deaf?"

THE "A" BOOK

"Maybe this special diet will help with your autism."

THE "A" BOOK

"You're a perfectly normal human being to me!"

"You are blessed with autism."

THE "A" BOOK

## ABOUT THE AUTHOR

Carissa Mordeno Paccerelli is a teen artist, illustrator, writer, and autism advocate. She has always had the proclivity to express herself through art. She started drawing when she was a toddler, but her art talent became evident at age three. Her artwork has been displayed in many exhibitions and won several awards and recognitions. At 15, she had her first solo exhibit hosted by the City of Pasadena Library.

In 2016, she represented the United States at the World Autism Festival in Vancouver, Canada, winning the First Place International Naturally Autistic People (INAP) Award for Visual Arts.

Carissa currently attends the Visual Arts & Design Academy (VADA) at Pasadena High School in California.

www.carissaspage.com